CELLS

CELLS

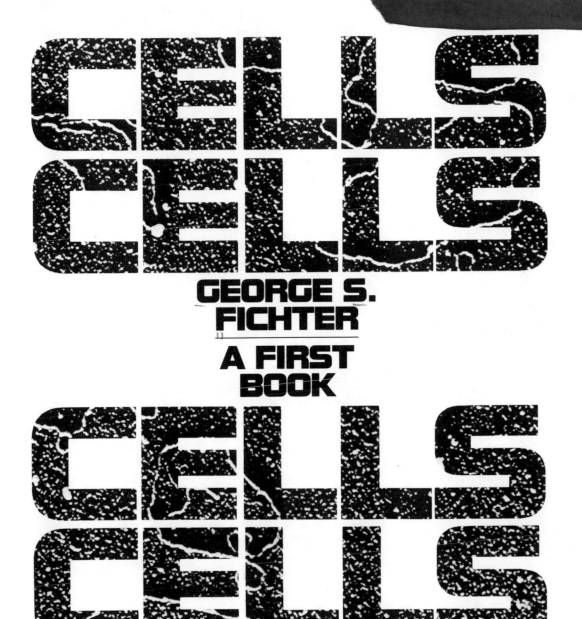

CELLS CELLS

GEORGE S. FICHTER

A FIRST BOOK

CELLS CELLS

Franklin Watts / New York / London / Toronto / Sydney / 1986

ARTWORK BY ANNE CANEVARI GREEN
Cover photograph courtesy of Michael R. Peres, RBP

Photographs courtesy of: Mary Evans Picture Library/Photo
Researchers: p. 11; J. F. Gennaro, L. R. Grillone, Cellular
Biology NYU/Photo Researchers: p. 12; Dr. Don Fawcett/Photo
Researchers: p. 24; Martin M. Rotker/Taurus Photos: pp. 25,
28, 36; Photo Researchers: p. 31; Biophoto Associates/Photo
Researchers: p. 42; Leonard Lee Rue III/Taurus Photos: p. 44;
D. W. Fawcett/D. Phillips/Science Source/Photo Researchers:
p. 53; AP/Wide World: pp. 56, 58 (top and bottom left), 61;
Alfred Owczarzak/Taurus Photos: p. 58 (right).

Library of Congress Cataloging-in-Publication Data

Fichter, George S.
Cells.

(A First Book)
Includes index.
Summary: Discusses the discovery of cells, their structure
and functions, and new experiments in DNA research.
1: Cells—Juvenile literature. [1. Cells]
1. Green, Anne Canevari, ill. 11. Title.
QH582.5.F53   1986   574.87   86-5667
ISBN 0-531-10210-6

CONTENTS

CELLS

CHAPTER ONE
BODY BUILDERS

The Smallest Units of Life

You began life as a single cell that weighed no more than a millionth of an ounce. Nine months later, when you were born, that single cell had become 2 trillion cells, and by that time you weighed six or seven pounds (3.1 kg). When you stop growing, your body will consist of about 100 trillion cells, and their total weight will be more than a hundred pounds (45 kg).

The individual cells that make up your body are too small to be seen with the naked eye. A thousand or more together would measure only an inch (2.5 cm) long. But it is cells that give your body its weight and shape. You look and act the way you do because of the different types of cells your body is composed of. And all of the information needed to form the different kinds of cells and trigger cell growth was coded in that single cell with which you started life.

Cells are the basic building blocks of your body. They are

the smallest organized units of nearly all living things. (Viruses and slime molds do not have distinct cells.) The simplest plants and animals live out their lives as single cells. They reproduce by dividing, the single cell becoming two. Many-celled plants and animals consist of various types of cells. Each type performs a different function and is dependent for survival on the work of other cells.

The Cell Theory

In 1660, Anton van Leeuwenhoek, a Dutch naturalist, used magnifying lenses to study a living world invisible to the naked eye. With his lenses, Leeuwenhoek could examine forms of life never before seen.

Other investigators were soon prying into this exciting new world. Five years later, Robert Hooke, an Englishman, examined a cut section of cork and gave the cavities he saw the name *cells,* meaning "little rooms." What he saw, of course, were empty spaces, like little boxes, but the name he gave them has persisted and is used today for the smallest fragments of organized living matter.

But it was not until 1839 that a true "cell theory" was developed. Two German scientists—Matthias Schleiden, a botanist, and Theodor Schwann, a zoologist—independently came to the conclusion that all living things are composed of one or more cells and that all cells are more or less alike and carry out similar functions to keep themselves alive. These conclusions had been reached earlier by other investigators, but Schleiden and Schwann were the first to put the findings together into a unified theory. Their work focused attention on cells as the basic units of all living things. Gradually it became clear that life today came from cells that were born in the distant past and will continue

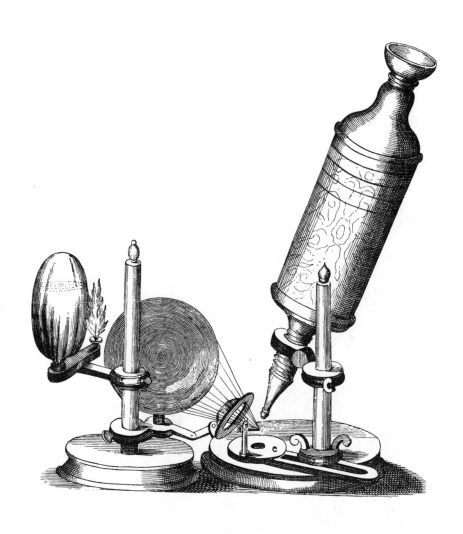

Hooke's microscope

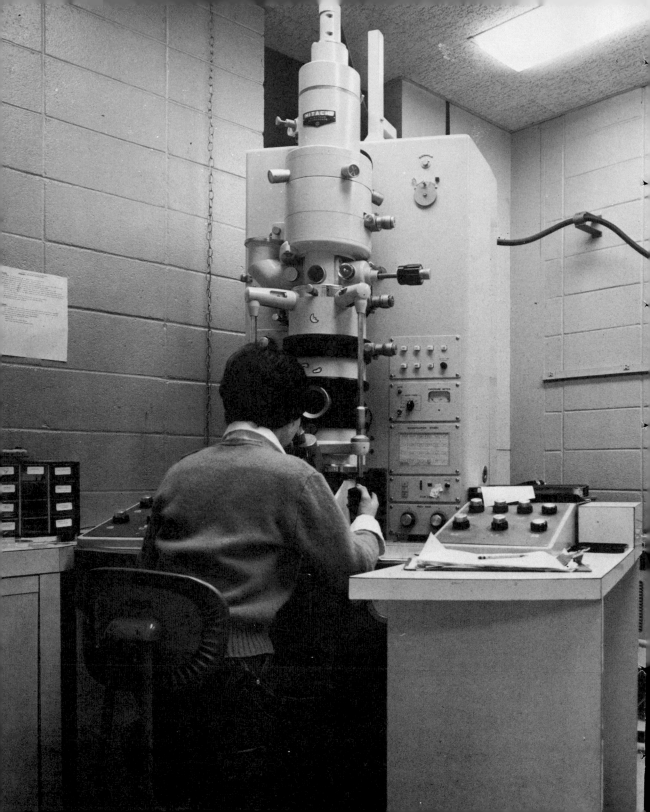

to form in the same way in the future. Through cells, life has continuity and even immortality, though the specific organism they make up will eventually die.

Leeuwenhoek designed some 250 different "microscopes" with which he studied the invisible worlds in water and elsewhere. Even the best of his microscopes were quite primitive; few of them could magnify objects more than 200 times. Modern scanning electron microscopes can achieve magnifications as great as 250,000 times. Scientists today are using these, as well as X rays and other techniques, to magnify and photograph living cells. The study of cells is called *cytology,* and scientists who specialize in the study of cells are called *cytologists*.

So while the key role played by cells as life's building blocks has been recognized for a century and a half, scientists are still probing their mysteries and getting ever closer looks at their inner workings.

A modern electron scanning microscope

CHAPTER TWO

A TYPICAL CELL

Nearly all cells share certain features.

A typical cell is enclosed in a sheath, or *cell membrane,* that holds the cell contents together. The cell membrane is not a solid wall, however. It is thin and semipermeable. Gases and fluids, plus whatever may be dissolved in them, can pass through it. This is how cells get oxygen for respiration and nutrients for growth. Carbon dioxide and other waste products pass out through the cell membrane.

In most cells, the cell membrane contains many folds or wrinkles—irregularities that increase the total surface area of the cell by many times. This allows for increased movement into, out of, and within the cell and permits more sites for chemical activity.

Some cells, such as white blood corpuscles, "eat" objects, such as invading bacteria, by surrounding them in an envelope-like fashion. Victims are caught in a pocket formed by folds in the cell membrane. The cell then digests what it has engulfed.

Inside the cell membrane is a grayish, jellylike substance called *cytoplasm*. The cytoplasm is almost clear near the outside of the cell but is denser and appears granular, like small pieces of sand, near the center of the cell. Although it consists of roughly 70 percent water, the cytoplasm also contains an amazing variety of other substances. Some are tiny structures called *organelles,* or "little organs." The cytoplasm also contains dissolved nutrients—proteins, which are the building blocks of the cell, plus sugars, starches, and fats, which provide energy. Finally, there are small amounts of salts, vitamins, and minerals. All of these substances interact within the cell. The precise chemical nature of this interaction varies according to the particular cell's function and its current state of activity.

Among the organelles are strands that form a network of "canals" extending throughout the cytoplasm. Some of these canals connect the *nucleus,* the control center of the cell, to the outer membrane; others join the various organelles. These strands, called the *endoplasmic reticulum,* are formed of the same substance as the cell membrane and serve as a supporting framework for the cell. They also serve as a circulatory system inside the cell, the cytoplasm "streaming," or moving about inside the cell, in an orderly pattern.

Among the organelles are important oval-shaped structures called *mitochondria.* Mitochondria are sometimes very plump and at other times very thin, their shape changing as conditions inside the cell change. Some cells contain more than a thousand of these little bodies, each of which has many inner folds that greatly increase the total surface area. Mitochondria are involved in the cell's respiration, which is the taking in of oxygen to burn food and generate energy. In the process, they also give off wastes, such as carbon dioxide and water. In a sense, mitochondria are the batteries on which the cell operates.

AN ANIMAL CELL

The tiny dots on the endoplasmic reticulum are **ribosomes,** which manufacture proteins.

The **cell membrane** controls the entrance and exit of molecules.

A watery substance called **cytoplasm** fills the cell.

The cell **nucleus** controls the activities of the cell and stores genetic information.

The **endoplasmic reticulum** transports materials around the cell.

A **mitochondrion** is the cell's power plant, where food is broken down to create energy.

The **Golgi apparatus** collects materials made in the cell for excretion.

The **nucleolus,** inside the nucleus, is responsible for making materials to repair the cell or to form a new cell.

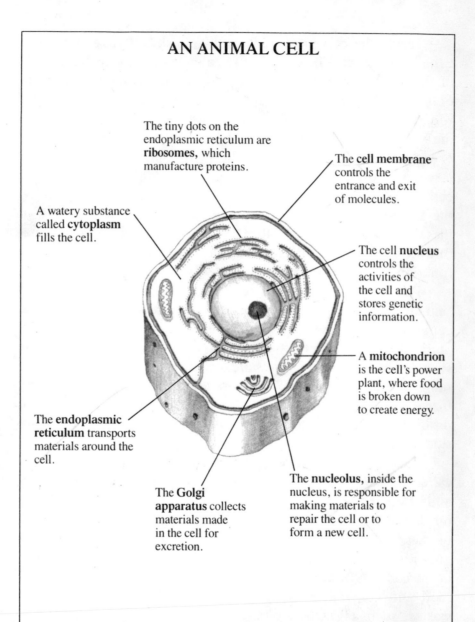

Lysosomes are small bodies rounder than mitochondria, but they do not have inner folds. Lysosomes contain chemicals called *enzymes,* which aid in the digestion of large food molecules. They also remove undigested wastes from the cytoplasm, moving to the surface of the cell and ejecting them.

Numerous tiny particles called *ribosomes* float freely throughout the cytoplasm or are attached to the membrane-like network of canals within the cell. Ribosomes help in the production of protein. Membranous sacs, called the *Golgi apparatus,* flat and stacked like pancakes, are packages of protein made by the ribosomes. These can be transported to wherever they are needed. Some cells contain a dozen or more of these structures. Also seen in nearly all cells is a rod-shaped structure called the *centriole.* The centriole is involved in cell division, or *reproduction.*

Throughout the cytoplasm of a typical cell are special pockets of fluid called *vacuoles.* Some vacuoles may also contain solid substances. Vacuoles are often seen where fluids or solids are being either taken into the cell or eliminated from it. A vacuole may be very small or, occasionally, as large as the cell itself, its size depending on the conditions inside the cell and the job the vacuole performs.

Usually found near the center of the cell is the nucleus. The nucleus controls the cell functions carried out by the organelles. It also contains the chemical substances that determine the inherited characteristics of the cell. The nearly round nucleus is much more dense than the cytoplasm and is enclosed by two layers of membrane. The outer layer is joined to the network of strands that runs throughout the cytoplasm and also to the outer cell membrane. The inner layer connects to the *nuclear sap,* which is much like the cytoplasm. Fine threads, called *chromatin,* run throughout the nuclear sap. When a cell is dividing, these

A PLANT CELL

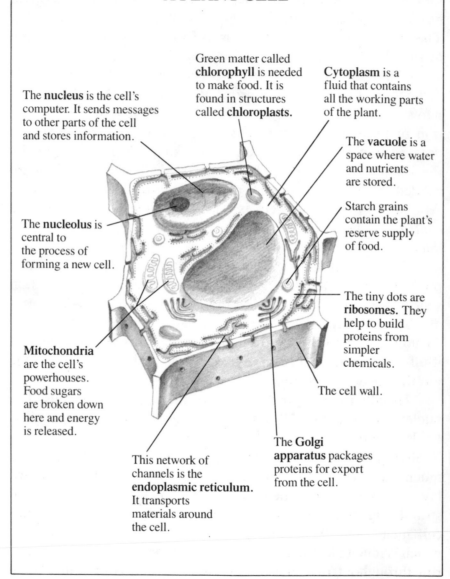

Green matter called **chlorophyll** is needed to make food. It is found in structures called **chloroplasts.**

Cytoplasm is a fluid that contains all the working parts of the plant.

The **nucleus** is the cell's computer. It sends messages to other parts of the cell and stores information.

The **vacuole** is a space where water and nutrients are stored.

Starch grains contain the plant's reserve supply of food.

The **nucleolus** is central to the process of forming a new cell.

The tiny dots are **ribosomes.** They help to build proteins from simpler chemicals.

Mitochondria are the cell's powerhouses. Food sugars are broken down here and energy is released.

The cell wall.

This network of channels is the **endoplasmic reticulum.** It transports materials around the cell.

The **Golgi apparatus** packages proteins for export from the cell.

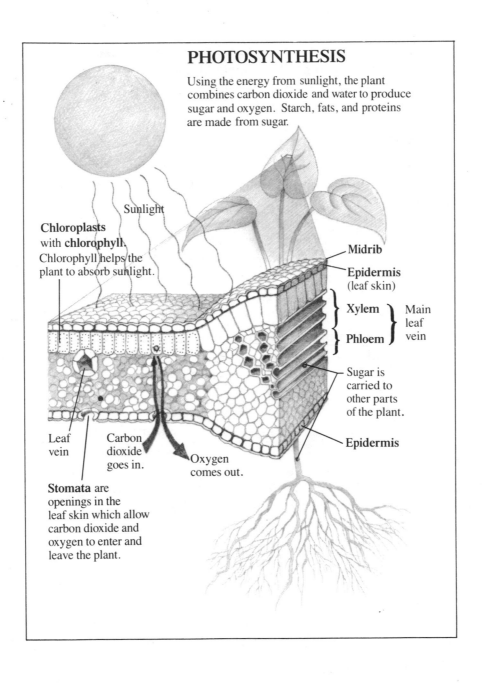

PHOTOSYNTHESIS

Using the energy from sunlight, the plant combines carbon dioxide and water to produce sugar and oxygen. Starch, fats, and proteins are made from sugar.

Sunlight

Chloroplasts with **chlorophyll**. Chlorophyll helps the plant to absorb sunlight.

Midrib

Epidermis (leaf skin)

Xylem

Phloem

Main leaf vein

Sugar is carried to other parts of the plant.

Epidermis

Leaf vein

Carbon dioxide goes in.

Oxygen comes out.

Stomata are openings in the leaf skin which allow carbon dioxide and oxygen to enter and leave the plant.

threads tighten to form the material that passes the cell's characteristics onto the two newly formed "daughter" cells.

Inside the nucleus of a typical cell, too, are one or more even denser round bodies called *nucleoli*. Nucleoli contain nuclear chemicals that play a role in protein synthesis.

Plant and animal cells are very similar, but there are some important differences. The vacuoles in plant cells are very large —filled with water and nutrients. Plant cells, in addition to the cell membrane, have a thick outer covering called the *cell wall*. The cell wall protects and supports the plant cell and remains intact even after the plant dies. In trees, the cell wall contains threads of cellulose, which are compacted into layers to form wood.

In the cytoplasm of plant cells are small green structures called *chloroplasts*, which contain molecules of the substance *chlorophyll*. Chlorophyll gives the plant the ability to make food. Making food, in fact, is the plant cell's major activity, and it is the major difference between plant and animal cells. Animal cells cannot produce their own food.

Thus, a cell is not a lifeless, jellylike blob. The cells in your body, like the cells in all living things, represent the very essence of life. Living things differ because they contain different types of cells, their cells are arranged differently, or their cells function a little differently. But the basic machinery operating all life is contained in cells that are essentially similar.

CHAPTER THREE
YOUR BODY'S SPECIAL CELLS

Your body consists of different types of cells. Those cells that look alike and that perform the same function form *tissues*—bone tissue, muscle tissue, skin tissue, nerve tissue, and so on. The shape of individual cells, in fact, is usually determined by the type of tissue the cells make up.

Different kinds of tissue often work together to form *organs*, and different organs work together to form body *systems*. Your stomach, for example, is an organ made up of several different kinds of tissue and is one of several organs that make up your digestive system. Other systems include the muscular, skeletal (bone), circulatory (blood), nervous, and respiratory (breathing) systems.

But the basic units of all these systems are tiny cells performing specific functions. Many of these cells are quite different from the typical cell described in the previous chapter.

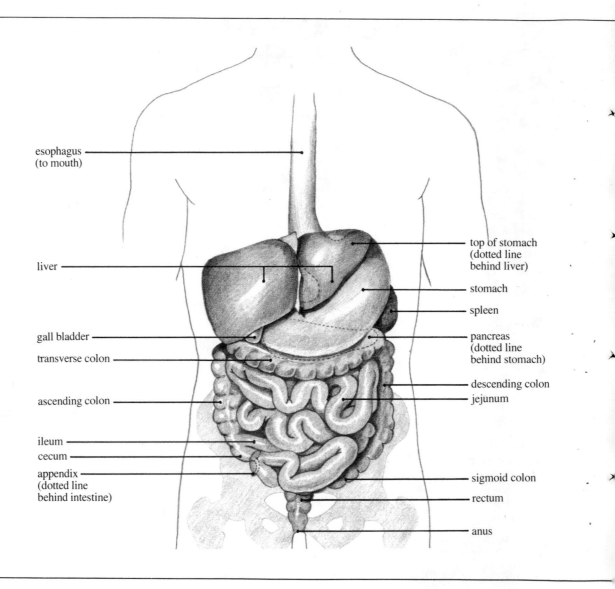

esophagus
(to mouth)

top of stomach
(dotted line
behind liver)

liver

stomach

spleen

gall bladder

pancreas
(dotted line
behind stomach)

transverse colon

descending colon

ascending colon

jejunum

ileum

cecum

appendix
(dotted line
behind intestine)

sigmoid colon

rectum

anus

The Digestive System

Muscle Cells

You have three kinds of muscles in your body. All share one feature: the ability to contract (shorten) and relax (lengthen). The more than 650 muscles in your body make movement possible. Some form a tight wrapping that holds your internal organs in place.

Walking, moving your arms, and turning your head are all forms of movement over which you have control, though you may perform these actions without much thought. The muscles that contract and relax in making these movements are called *voluntary,* or *skeletal, muscles.* Another name for them is *striated muscles,* for if you examine fibers of this muscle tissue under a microscope, you will discover that they are made up of elongated, striped cells. The stripes consist of bands of protein. Each muscle cell also contains many nuclei.

Striated muscles allow for quick movement, but they tire easily and must be rested. You can build up strength in them by exercising. Exercise increases the size of the muscle cells, but the number of muscle cells in your body remains the same throughout your life. Striated muscles account for 40 to 50 percent of your body's weight. They include the big gluteus maximus forming your buttocks and muscles as much as 12 inches (30 cm) long in your upper leg.

Smooth muscles react more sluggishly than do the striated muscles, but they can continue to work over a longer period of time without rest. The spindle-shaped cells of smooth muscles contain only one nucleus, and they do not appear striped.

Because we have only very limited or no control over their action, these muscles are also called *involuntary muscles.* They are found in your blood vessels, the walls of your stomach and intestines, the irises of your eyes, and elsewhere throughout your

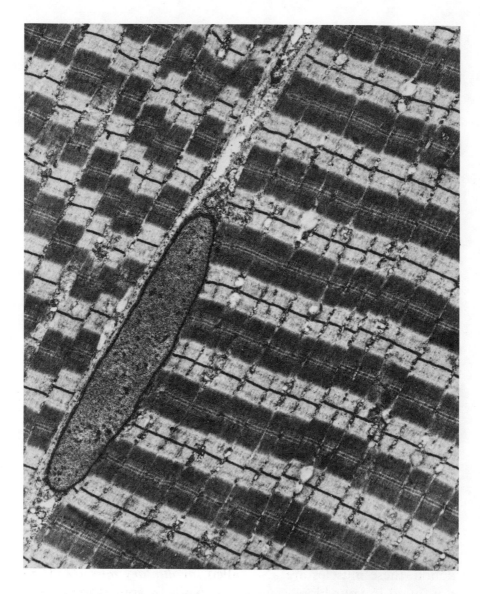

*Striated muscle. Note the bands of
protein running throughout.*

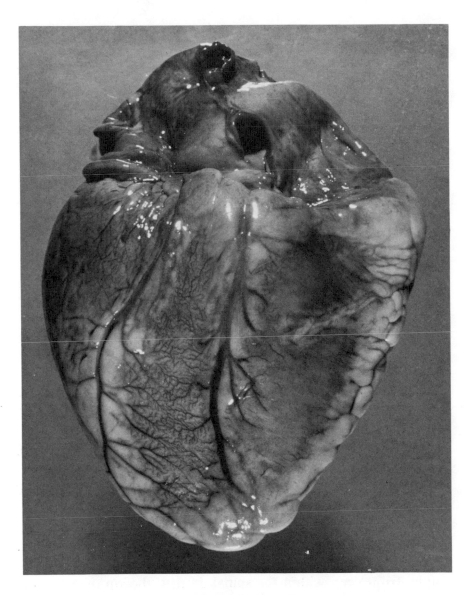

*A frontal view of
the human heart*

body. Smooth muscles are automatically stimulated into action by nerves and by changes in your body's chemistry.

The heart is the hardest working muscle in your body. Though it is an involuntary muscle, the cells forming its fibers have many nuclei, like the striated muscle cells.

Your remarkable heart beats 60 to 80 times a minute every minute of every day for as long as you live. And every day it pumps about 1,250 gallons (4,700 l) of blood throughout your body. If you had to think to make your heart beat, you could never sleep, and you would have no time to do anything else while you were awake.

Nerve Cells

We are born with all the nerve cells, or *neurons,* we will ever have. They do not increase in number and are capable of very limited repair. But there are plenty of them—billions of nerve cells in the brain, spinal cord, and throughout the body. They form a complex communications network unmatched by any electronic system so far devised. The nervous system controls what we see, hear, taste, touch, and feel, and how we think and respond to different situations.

Each nerve cell contains a single nucleus. Reaching out from the cell body are branches, or fibers, of varying lengths. These fibers, called *dendrites,* transmit signals, or impulses, from outside to the cell body. A nerve cell may have a hundred or more dendrites, though the number is usually lower.

Signals are carried away from the cell body by a fiber called an *axon*. This single fiber can extend great distances, for example, from deep within the spinal cord to the tip of a toe—a distance of 3 feet (0.9 m) or more. It is axons that make nerve cells some of the longest cells in the body.

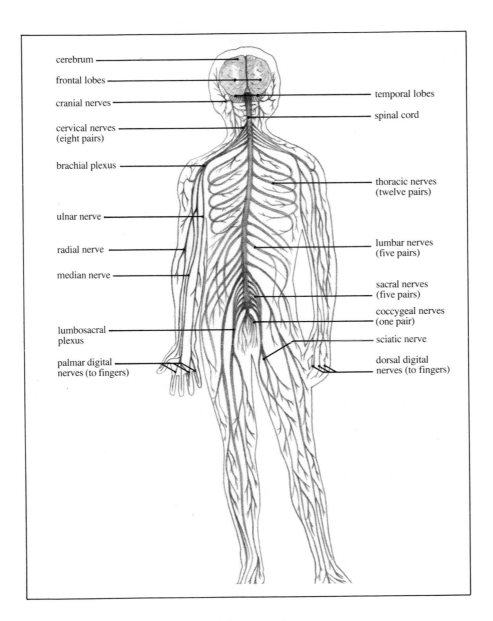

cerebrum

frontal lobes

cranial nerves

cervical nerves
(eight pairs)

brachial plexus

ulnar nerve

radial nerve

median nerve

lumbosacral
plexus

palmar digital
nerves (to fingers)

temporal lobes

spinal cord

thoracic nerves
(twelve pairs)

lumbar nerves
(five pairs)

sacral nerves
(five pairs)

coccygeal nerves
(one pair)

sciatic nerve

dorsal digital
nerves (to fingers)

The Nervous System

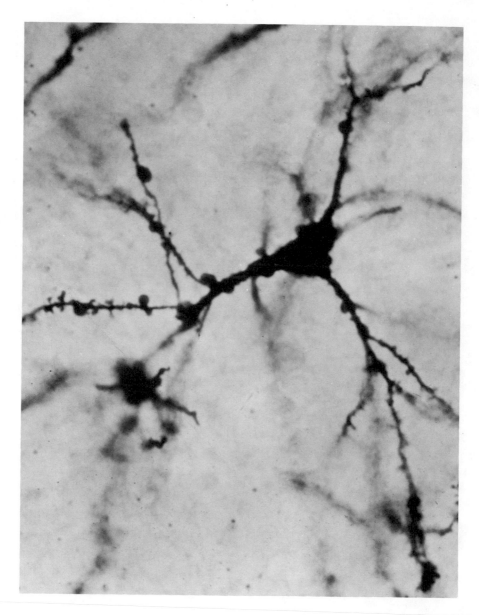

Nerve cells from the human brain

Bundles of nerve fibers are called *nerves*. Nerve fibers are usually covered by a layer of fatty material, like the wrapping around electrical wire. Signals travel much more rapidly in nerve fibers because of this covering.

Sensory nerves receive information from the environment. If you touch a flame, for example, a sensory nerve cell picks up the "pain" as information and transmits it rapidly to a motor nerve cell. Messages travel through nerves as rapidly as 450 feet (130 m) per second.

Both dendrites and axons end in a brush of tiny fibers. Dendrites may end in sensory terminals, such as taste buds. Dendrite endings in the tips of your fingers give you the sensation of touch. Your skin, in fact, has some 50 miles (78 km) of nerves that constantly report on the world around you. Many axons end at muscle fibers, triggering them into action.

The tiny branches of the nerve cells come very close but do not touch each other. The transmission—actually an electrical impulse—is passed over this microscopic gap, or *synapse*, by chemicals.

Your brain and spinal cord, forming the central nervous system, consist of large masses of nerve cells. They are the most complex portion of your nervous system, and they form your body's master control center. Your body contains an estimated 10 billion or more nerve cells. Over half of these are located in the cerebrum, the largest portion of your brain.

Your brain controls most of your actions. You think about what you want to do, then your brain transmits the message to the proper place for action. You literally command your arm to lift, for example, though this is done so quickly you may not recognize it as a thought action.

But your brain also controls involuntary actions, such as the beating of your heart. An adult brain weighs only about 3 pounds (1.35 kg), which is roughly 2 percent of body weight. But the brain utilizes nearly 25 percent of the energy produced by the body. Thinking burns fuel more rapidly and in greater amounts than you might imagine!

Your spinal cord runs through the hollow cavity of your backbone. This gives it a protective covering just as your brain is housed in a protective bony skull. Nerve cells in your spinal cord send messages to and from your brain. But the spinal cord also serves as a shortcut, or reflex center, for messages that need immediate attention, such as withdrawing a hand from a hot flame.

Blood Cells

Your body contains about 6 quarts (5.7 l) of blood that is circulated constantly by your heart. Blood pumped from the heart moves through major arteries into smaller and smaller blood vessels. These blood vessels open into tiny capillaries. Capillaries have small openings that allow gases and chemicals to pass into and out of the watery fluid, or *lymph,* that bathes your body's cells.

Blood coming from the heart carries oxygen and nutrients to the cells. Once the delivery is completed, water and carbon dioxide move through the lymph and back into the capillaries, then into veins, before completing the trip back to the heart. From the heart the returned blood takes a short trip to the lungs, where the carbon dioxide picked up as a waste from the cells is exchanged for a new supply of oxygen. The blood is then ready for another trip around the body. Blood is, in effect, a circulating tissue.

Much of the blood consists of a yellowish "plasma" that is roughly 90 percent water. But in this fluid are countless cells.

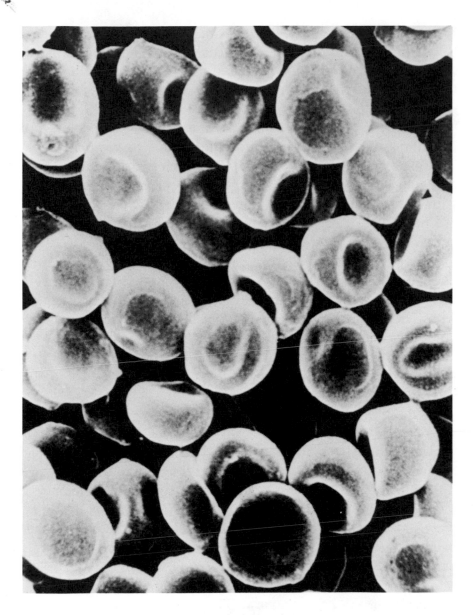

Red blood cells

Most numerous are the *red blood cells*. These transport oxygen to the body's cells and take away carbon dioxide. It has been estimated that your blood contains as many as 25 billion red blood cells and that their total surface area is about 1,500 times greater than the outer surface area of your body.

Individual red blood cells are yellowish orange in color, but in clumps they are red. The red color is due to *hemoglobin*, a substance made of protein and iron that can contain great amounts of oxygen. Blood coming directly from the heart is rich with oxygen and bright red. When an artery is cut, this bright red blood spurts out with each beat of the heart. Blood from a vein is not as red, and it flows more slowly.

New red blood cells are produced constantly in the red marrow of the long bones in your body. A mature red blood cell does not have a nucleus. It is round and has ballooned edges, with a depression in the middle—much like a doughnut with its hole not completely punched out. During its life of about 120 days, a red blood cell travels more than 1,000 miles (640 km) through the bloodstream. Then it becomes useless and is reabsorbed by the body.

Along with the red blood cells are *white blood cells,* or *leucocytes*. These are much fewer in number—only about one white blood cell for every 5,000 red blood cells, though their number may increase if there is a need for them in the body.

White blood cells are two or three times larger than red blood cells. They have nuclei but no color. They move about like one-celled amoebas, across capillary walls into the lymph and back again, and they perform the important function of "eating" bacteria and other invaders.

Platelets, which are really just cell fragments, are produced constantly in the bone marrow. They have a short life but an important job—they release a substance that helps blood to clot. This is important when you cut yourself. It is platelets that help to stop the bleeding.

Bone Cells

By the time you were born, most of the 206 bones in your body were already fully formed. They continue to grow, however, until you are 16 to 18 years old if you are a girl, 18 to 21 years old if you are a boy. Bones form the body's skeleton. They protect delicate nerves and provide "hitching posts" for muscles.

Bone is a living tissue. A bone will mend itself if it is broken. If the sections of the break are lined up carefully and then held in place by splints or a cast, they will grow together again and the bone will be as strong as it was originally. This mending occurs very rapidly when you are young. It takes longer when you are grown.

Bone is produced by cells called *osteocytes,* which secrete a protein material in which minerals—particularly calcium carbonate and calcium phosphate—are deposited. These minerals account for about 65 percent of a bone's weight. When a person is very young, there are lesser amounts of minerals, and the bones will often bend without breaking. As a person grows older, mineral deposits increase. In old age, a person's bones may become quite brittle from an overabundance of minerals, causing the bones to break easily.

A typical long bone, such as your upper arm bone (humerus) or your thigh bone (femur), has a thin, tough covering to which your muscles and tendons are attached. This covering also contains bone cells that begin their repair work immediately if the bone is cracked or broken.

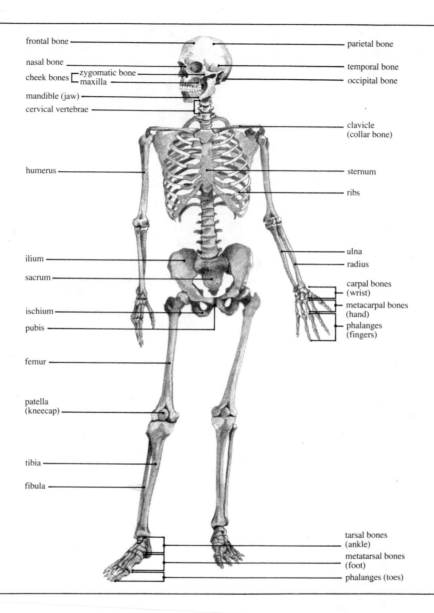

frontal bone ————————————— parietal bone

nasal bone ———————————— temporal bone

cheek bones ⌈ zygomatic bone ————————— occipital bone
            ⌊ maxilla

mandible (jaw) ————————————

cervical vertebrae ————————

clavicle
(collar bone)

humerus ————————————— sternum

ribs

ilium ——————————— ulna

sacrum ————————————— radius

carpal bones
(wrist)

ischium ——————————— metacarpal bones
                        (hand)

pubis ———————————— phalanges
                        (fingers)

femur ———————————

patella
(kneecap) —————————————

tibia ——————————

fibula ————————————

tarsal bones
(ankle)

metatarsal bones
(foot)

phalanges (toes)

The Skeletal System

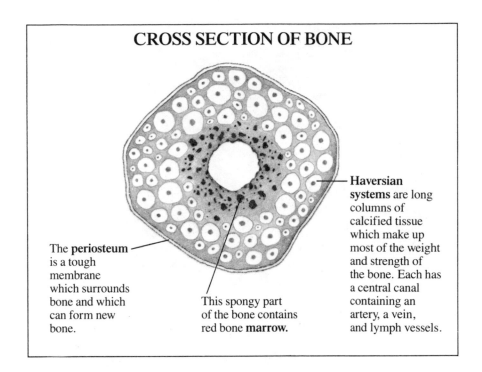

CROSS SECTION OF BONE

The **periosteum** is a tough membrane which surrounds bone and which can form new bone.

This spongy part of the bone contains red bone **marrow.**

Haversian systems are long columns of calcified tissue which make up most of the weight and strength of the bone. Each has a central canal containing an artery, a vein, and lymph vessels.

Directly beneath this covering is the hard or compact bone, containing a network of blood vessels. This is the bone in which living bone cells have deposited the minerals.

Under this hard bone and especially toward the ends of the long bones is a layer of spongy bone. The many spaces in the spongy bone make it light in weight. These spaces are filled in with the red marrow that produces red blood cells, white blood cells, and blood platelets. In the hollow center of bones is a yellowish, fatty marrow.

Teeth are a special kind of bone. Teeth cannot heal themselves as other bones do, but they are covered with enamel, the

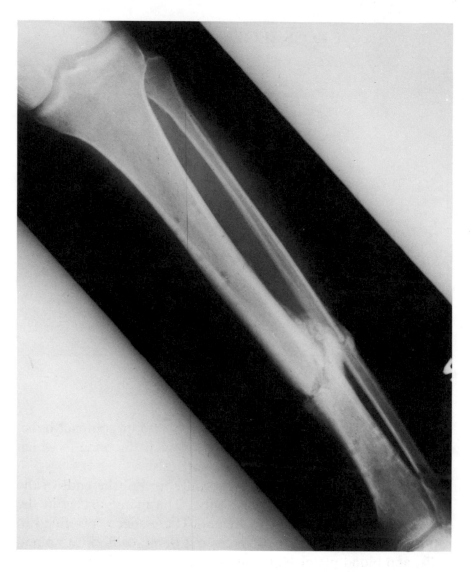

*A healing fracture of a human tibia and fibula
(the leg). Note the calcification around the break
as the bone fragments "weld" together.*

hardest substance in your body. Enamel consists almost entirely of minerals—mostly calcium carbonate and calcium phosphate, like the other bones in the body.

Skin Cells

The bony skeleton is your body's framework, and muscles give your body its shape. Covering the outside of your body—its wrapper, so to speak—is your skin. It is your body's largest and most spread-out organ. No other organ in your body grows as rapidly, and lost skin cells are replaced throughout your life.

Your skin is thinnest over your eyeballs and thickest on the soles of your feet. Altogether the billions of cells forming your skin weigh about 7 pounds (3.1 kg) and, if stretched out, would cover an area of nearly 20 square feet (1.8 sq. m).

Skin gets its color from a pigment called *melanin*. Dark or brown-skinned people have a lot of melanin in their skin. People with white skin have very little melanin. Freckles are spots of melanin in the skin. When people get suntans, they are causing the skin to produce melanin as a protection from burning. If they become sunburned, the outer layer of skin peels off.

Your skin's outer layer, or *epidermis*, consists mostly of dead cells. Millions of these cells are shed every day. The epidermis is covered with a thin layer of oil secreted by cells in the inner layer, or *dermis*. The oil keeps your skin soft and also makes it waterproof.

New skin cells are produced constantly by the dermis. In this thick, deeper layer, too, are the roots of the hairs on your body. Hair consists of dead cells, but hair roots are alive. In total, you have about 250,000 hairs on your body. At the base of each hair is a tiny muscle that can literally lift up the hair—make it "stand on end," as when you are frightened.

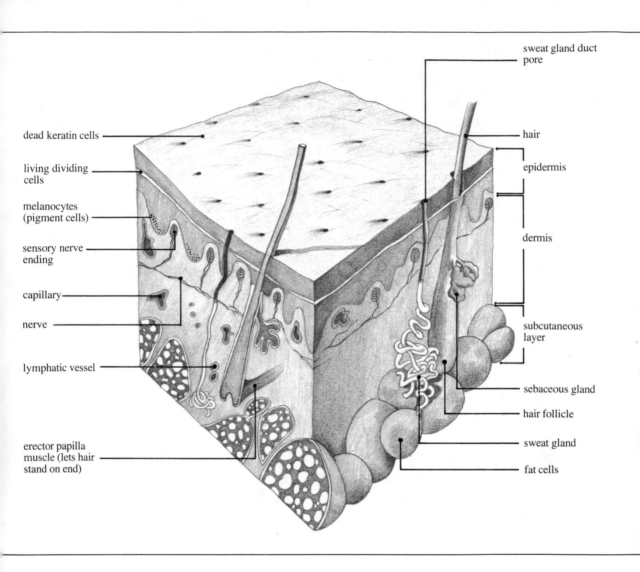

dead keratin cells

living dividing cells

melanocytes (pigment cells)

sensory nerve ending

capillary

nerve

lymphatic vessel

erector papilla muscle (lets hair stand on end)

sweat gland duct pore

hair

epidermis

dermis

subcutaneous layer

sebaceous gland

hair follicle

sweat gland

fat cells

Cross Section of Skin

The thick layers of the dermis give your skin ridges. These form your fingerprints, which are unique—no one else has fingerprints to match yours. Your fingernails and toenails are also outgrowths of the dermis.

Nerve endings in your skin are sensitive to heat, cold, pressure, and pain. The skin also contains a layer of fat that helps to insulate your body—keep it warm.

Sweat glands in the skin help regulate the body's temperature, too. The sweat glands open up on hot days and release water and salts—waste materials—from the cells. Evaporation of the fluids cools your body. On cold days, the sweat glands stay closed, and when you don't perspire, your body stays warm. Tiny blood vessels in your skin also help in keeping you either cool or warm. If you are hot, the blood vessels expand. This brings them closer to the surface, where they can radiate heat away from your body. In cool weather they shrink and stay deep in your skin.

Your body contains many other specialized cells. Some secrete *hormones,* which are special chemicals that regulate certain bodily activities. Other cells produce digestive enzymes released in the stomach and intestines. Still others are specially developed for sensing physical and chemical changes in the body. In a later chapter, we will look at another, very important type of cell—the sex cell, which permits cell reproduction to occur.

You are indeed an incredible accumulation of specialized cells. And all of them work together to make you what you are.

CHAPTER FOUR

HOW CELLS SURVIVE AND DO WORK

Every living cell in your body needs oxygen and nutrients to survive and do its work. The oxygen comes from your lungs, and the nutrients are supplied by the foods you eat. Both are carried to your cells by your blood.

How Cells "Eat"

Cells cannot digest a hamburger, a salad, or a milkshake, of course. Your digestive system works on these foods to reduce them to substances your cells can use for growth and energy. Starting in your mouth and continuing through the small intestine, foods are broken down, or digested, by digestive juices and enzymes, until they are tiny molecules. These molecules move out of the digestive tract into the blood and then pass through the cell membrane into the cell.

Foods containing starches and complex sugars—the carbohydrates—are changed into simple sugars. In the cells, these sugars are "burned" to release energy. The "burning" is strictly a chemical reaction, of course. There is no flame or smoke, and very little heat is given off. The energy produced is released slowly and steadily or is immediately stored in another chemical form.

Fats are another high-energy food. We get fats from such foods as ice cream, milk, meats, eggs, and nuts. Some fat is used immediately by the cells as a source of energy. The rest is stored in the body for later use. Stored fats provide insulation, serve as protective cushions for the muscles and nerves, and prop up some body organs, including the kidneys.

But the cell's energy batteries are the plump, sausage-shaped mitochondria. It is in these structures that energy is produced, by the combining of oxygen with sugar molecules. The energy released is converted into chemical energy and stored temporarily in the form of a molecule called *ATP* (adenosine triphosphate). This molecule is found in all living cells where energy is needed. All of these reactions depend on oxygen carried to the cells by the red blood cells. Carbon dioxide and water are given off as wastes. The chemical changes that take place in the living cell are collectively known as the body's *metabolism*.

Proteins, which we get from fish, meat, eggs, milk, and some fruits and vegetables, are broken down by digestion into their basic units, *amino acids*. Like other foods, proteins contain carbon, hydrogen, and oxygen, but they also contain nitrogen. In the cells, the amino acids are reconstructed to become the basic building blocks for your muscles and other body parts. Unlike fat, protein is not stored in the body. It must be supplied daily.

Most of the work done by your cell "factories" in making proteins takes place in the ribosomes that are scattered throughout the cell. These granule-like structures are directed by the cell nucleus to produce specific kinds of protein from the amino acids

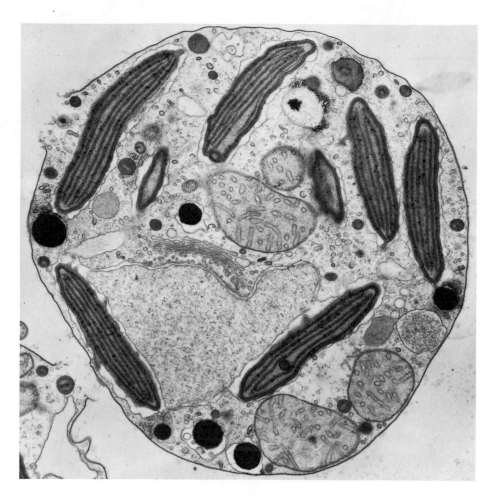

A plant cell (from the yellow-green algae
Tribonema vulgare) *showing eight chloroplasts*
(elongated, dark objects), several mitochondria
(lighter, round or oval-shaped objects), and
a large nucleus (lower left). The picture,
an electron micrograph, shows a cell that
has been magnified 24,000 times.

supplied to the cell. (We'll discuss this in more detail in the next chapter.) Some of the proteins produced are used by the cell itself. Others are transported to other cells throughout the body.

In addition to fairly large amounts of these basic nutrients, cells need smaller amounts of vitamins and minerals to operate properly.

Not all cells need the same kinds or amounts of nutrients. Bone cells, for example, need iron for making red blood cells. They also need calcium carbonate, calcium phosphate, and other minerals for their own maintenance.

Aging and Death of Cells

A snake may get a new skin several times a year. As the snake grows, its skin becomes too tight, and when this happens, a new skin begins to form underneath. When the new skin is ready, the snake rubs against a rock or some other hard object to loosen the old skin around its mouth and nose and then simply crawls out of it, much as you might take off a sweater. The old skin is left behind, often completely intact.

You may have heard that you get a completely new covering of skin every seven years. But you don't crawl out of your old skin, as the snake does. Old skin cells die and flake off constantly and are replaced by new skin cells.

Cells do indeed age and die. Some kinds are replaced, but others are not. Your muscle cells, for example, grow along with you, but they are capable of only limited repair and replacement. Nerve cells are even less able to repair themselves. Generally, once they are destroyed, they are gone forever. In contrast, red blood cells—and there may be 100 million of them in a drop of blood—wear out regularly and are replaced by new ones at the rate of about 2 million every second.

A snake shedding its skin

Scientists estimate that as much as 2 percent of the cells in the human body die every day. Billions of cells must be produced to replace them. If you are still growing, more cells are produced than are lost each day. Or, if a portion of your body is cut or damaged, the rate of repair is accelerated to match the need.

Death occurs when cells stop functioning and reproducing. We'll see in the next chapter how, in sexually reproducing organisms, immortality—at least a form of it—is achieved through the uniting of sex cells to produce offspring that exhibit certain likenesses to each parent.

CHAPTER FIVE
HOW CELLS REPRODUCE

Cell Division

Every cell in your body came from another cell. Most cells, in fact, can reproduce themselves again and again, with each daughter cell an exact duplicate of the parent cell from which it came. This division process is called *mitosis*.

A cell spends more than half of its time in what is called the "resting" stage. The cell is not really resting, of course. Rather, this is the time when it carries on its normal functions. The cell is "resting" only in that it is not reproducing itself.

During its resting stage, a cell becomes organized internally, making ready for its division. The cell duplicates its threads of chromatin in the nucleus. When the cell is mature and division is about to occur, these threads thicken and form *chromosomes* that divide into sets of identical pairs. At the same time, the membrane around the nucleus disappears.

The chromosomes line up in the middle of the cell. Then

each one separates from its duplicate copy and moves along rays, or spindle fibers, that form when the centriole divides. The chromosome halves are now situated at the opposite ends of the cell. After the chromosomes arrive at the ends of the cell, the spindle fibers break down, and a membrane forms around each chromosome group. Two new nuclei are formed. A crease now forms in the middle of the cell, pinching it into two distinct daughter cells. Each new cell is identical to its parent but about half as large.

Occasionally—but very rarely—a cell does not get the same chromosome parts as its parents, or it may get them in a jumbled order. These abnormal cells that do not have the proper genetic makeup are called *mutants*. Usually they are unable to perform properly and are short-lived, but sometimes mutants do survive. If they happen to be better suited to their environment than the parent cell, they can start a complete change in the inheritance pattern.

How long does it take for a cell to divide? Many cells go through the entire process in less than an hour. Others regularly take three hours or even longer. The starting of the process and the length of time it takes is coded into the cell. Cells do not, for example, divide so rapidly that they become smaller and smaller. Rather, a cell does not usually divide until it "matures"—that is, reaches its full size. The two smaller cells that result from the division then grow in size before they divide.

Sex Cells

One-celled plant-like and animal-like organisms duplicate themselves, or reproduce, by simply dividing and becoming two separate organisms. The division is by mitosis, or a modified form of mitosis. In many-celled plants and animals, the reproductive

MITOSIS

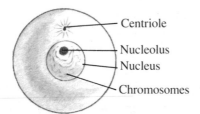

Centriole

Nucleolus

Nucleus

Chromosomes

1. This is a cell as it appears before mitosis begins.

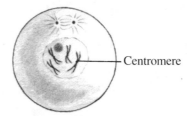

Centromere

2. The cell is now preparing to divide. The chromosomes become distinct bodies in the nucleus, with a split along their length, held together in the middle by the **centromere.** Meanwhile, the centriole divides and separates, throwing out a radiating system of protein fibers.

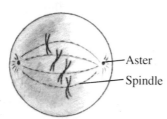

Aster

Spindle

3. The two radiating systems formed by the splitting of the centriole are now called **asters,** and they travel to opposite sides of the cell. They then become connected by fibers into a system called the **spindle.**

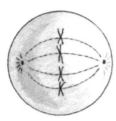

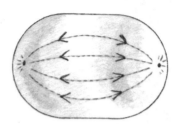

4. The chromosomes arrange themselves along the equator of the spindle, midway between the two asters (centrioles).

5. The chromosomes divide completely, and each set of daughter chromosomes migrates to each pole. The cell begins to divide in two.

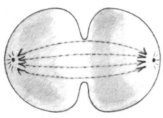

6. The entire cell divides. Animal cells do this by pinching in two (as shown here), and plant cells do it by building a new wall.

7. Two identical daughter cells have been formed, each with the same number of chromosomes as the parent cell.

MEIOSIS (Cell division that forms the sex cells)

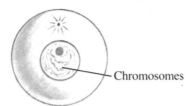 Chromosomes

1. The cell as it appears before meiosis. The chromosomes are not distinct.

2. The 46 chromosomes appear as distinct bodies in the nucleus. (Only 4 chromosomes are shown here).

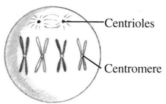 Centrioles

Centromere

3. The chromosomes split (double) along their length, exactly as in mitosis, held together in the center by **centromeres.** Meanwhile, the centriole has divided and each new centriole has started to move to opposite sides of the cell.

4. Double chromosomes that are similar line up next to each other, with some of their parts overlapping and "sticking" to each other.

5. The double chromosomes separate from each other and line up at the center of the cell. When they separate, the chromosomes take pieces of each other with them. This is called "**crossing over.**"

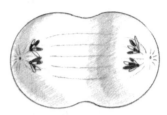

6. The double chromosomes are then pulled to opposite poles of the cell. The cell begins to divide in two.

7. The original cell splits into two new cells. Each contains 23 double non-identical chromosomes. (Only 2 are shown here).

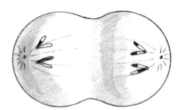

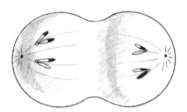

8. The double chromosomes in each cell split apart. Each half, known as a **chromatid**, is pulled to the side of the cell. The cells begin again to divide in two.

9. Each cell splits to form two new cells, called **gametes**. A gamete contains 23 chromatids. In **fertilization**, two gametes join to form a new cell, called a **zygote**, which contains the full set of 46 chromosomes.

process is more complicated. These organisms produce special "sex" cells, called *gametes*. Gametes produced by females are called *eggs*. Gametes produced by males are called *sperm*. An egg and a sperm unite to form a *zygote*, which grows into a new individual.

Sex cells differ from "body" cells (most cells in the body) in their number of chromosomes. Human body cells contain 46 chromosomes. In *genetics,* the branch of science concerned with heredity, this full quota of chromosomes is called the *diploid number*. Sex cells contain half this number of chromosomes— the *monoploid,* or *haploid, number*.

Why do sex cells have only half as many chromosomes as do body cells? Because when the sperm and egg unite, which is called *fertilization*, each contributes its half-set of chromosomes to the fertilized egg, or zygote. Thus, the zygote ends up with the normal, or diploid, number of chromosomes.

Sex cells are produced by a special kind of division called *meiosis*. This division resembles mitosis except for what happens to the chromosomes. Each chromosome first duplicates, as in mitosis, and similarly shaped chromosomes line up in the middle of the cell. Each of these pairs of chromosomes has four strands. The cell divides twice, separating the pairs of chromosomes and then again separating the duplicated threads into four new cells. Each of the four cells contains half the number of chromosomes as body cells.

In males, each of the newly created sex cells becomes a sperm. At any particular time, an adult male may have literally millions of sperm in his body. In females, similar divisions take place, but only one of the four cells becomes an egg. The others disintegrate. A human female produces only one egg at a time, approximately every 28 days.

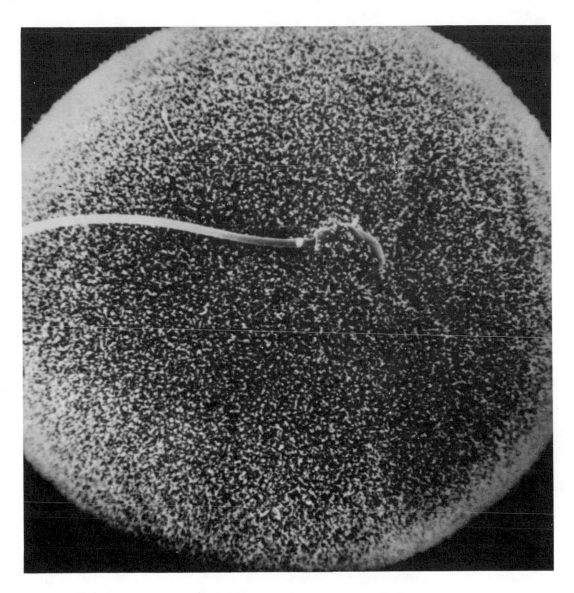

A sperm penetrating an egg during fertilization

The simplest creatures reproduce themselves through *asexual reproduction*. When an amoeba (a one-celled animal) divides, the two new cells are exactly like the parent cell in genetic makeup. In *sexual reproduction,* a sperm and an egg from two different parents unite. Each parent contributes a different set of characteristics.

Because so many variations are possible with sexual reproduction, no two individuals are exactly alike. (The only exceptions are identical siblings—twins, triplets, and so on—which are produced by a divided fertilized egg.) Offspring may resemble neither parent. For example, both parents may have brown eyes. Each parent, however, may carry a *gene* (the unit that passes along traits) for blue eyes that is masked, or dominated, by the gene for brown eyes. It is possible for each of these parents to contribute to the zygote the gene for blue eyes, however, and if this happens to occur in the same zygote, their child will have blue eyes. We'll talk more about the processes that make each person unique in the next chapter.

CHAPTER SIX

WHAT MAKES YOU UNIQUE

Unless you have an identical twin, no one in the world is precisely like you—nor will ever be. Identical siblings are exceptions because each child originates from the same fertilized egg and thus has the same genetic makeup.

Coded into the single cell that started your life was all the information necessary to enable you to talk, sing, dance, read, feel emotions, and do the many other things that make you a person. Your similarities to other people, as well as what makes you unique, were programmed into spirals of a substance called *DNA*, which was present in the fertilized egg from which you developed.

DNA (deoxyribonucleic acid) is the ultimate marvel of cells. It is DNA that makes a simple cell a marvel of sophistication, enabling cells to change a few raw materials into literally thousands of different chemical products that perform specific roles in life.

For more than a hundred years, scientists have recognized a relationship between chromosomes and heredity. More recently they could see in their microscopes that each daughter cell received the same number of chromosomes—one apiece from identical pairs produced when the cell divided. As microscopes grew in their powers of magnification, beadlike chains could be seen in the chromosomes. These were the genes; a single chromosome consists of thousands of them. It became generally accepted that genes were responsible for particular features or characteristics. In other words, genes controlled the color of your hair or eyes, how tall you would become, and so on.

When scientists began to probe the structure of the genes, they discovered that the chemical makeup of genes was DNA. But they did not understand how DNA molecules were linked. Two young scientists—James Watson and Francis Crick—arrived at the answer in the early 1950s. In so doing, they ushered in a whole new era of biology.

Watson and Crick knew from the work of other scientists what materials DNA consisted of. They determined the exact structure of the DNA by using X rays and making models in which the parts could be juggled until they were in the proper arrangement. A DNA molecule, they concluded, consists of a twisted spiral (or ladder) called by scientists a *double helix*. Phosphate and sugar strands form the sides of the ladder, and four kinds of nitrogen bases (adenine, thymine, guanine, and

Twins, Leo and Leon Viall, who still look alike even in their advanced years. Both men are widowers, retired dentists, and live in Avon Park, Florida.

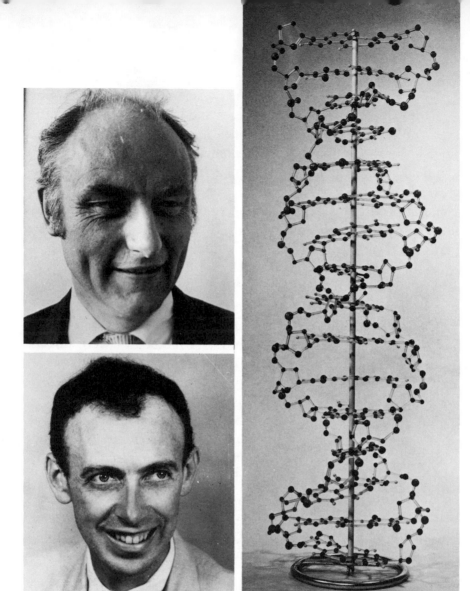

Drs. Francis Crick (top) and James Watson, joint winners of the 1962 Nobel Prize for Medicine for their work in discovering the double helix (spiral ladder— see replica at right) structure of DNA.

cytosine) form the rungs. Further, the nitrogen bases always pair up in the same way—adenine with thymine and guanine with cytosine. The pairs are joined very weakly, and so the strands can be broken apart easily, or "unzipped," down the middle.

This is precisely what occurs, in fact, when a cell divides. Each daughter cell gets an exact duplicate of the DNA in the parent cell.

DNA contains the information for putting together the amino acids that are the basic building blocks of proteins. There are 20 different kinds of amino acids, and in the human body, these can be arranged into many different kinds of proteins, including the enzymes. There are some 30,000 different proteins in your body, for example. The particular combinations of the pairs of nitrogen bases in the DNA—the DNA code—determines which protein will be made.

Messages are sent from the cell's nucleus to the ribosomes in the cell's cytoplasm by still another substance—*RNA*. RNA is chemically quite similar to DNA but consists only of a single strand of sugar. "Messenger" RNA molecules transmit their information to yet another kind of RNA molecule—"transfer" RNA—in the ribosome. The proper kinds of amino acids are matched up to form the correct protein. The reactions are precise and complex, but a cell can link up nearly a hundred amino acids in this manner every minute.

Sex cells, we learned earlier, contain only half as many chromosomes as do body cells. Each parent contributes half of the DNA that is in the fertilized egg. Each sex cell contains 25,000 or more genes randomly selected in the division that produced it. The combining of the two sex cells results in a genetic makeup that is unique. And all of the information necessary to put this information into action is contained in the DNA of a single cell. Language simply cannot express how remarkable this is.

CHAPTER SEVEN

DAWN OF A NEW ERA

With their new knowledge of the DNA molecule, scientists were equipped to start a revolution in biology. Could living things be manipulated to change their genetic makeup?

Indeed they could.

The DNA molecule in a single cell in your body measures up to 3 feet (0.9 m) long. Each cell contains many such strands, and you have as many as 100 trillion cells in your body. The countless microscopic strands of DNA they contain could stretch to the sun and back. (Interestingly, there are many blank spaces, containing no coded information, along the strands.)

All of this DNA was produced from one master plan in the single cell that started your life. Changes made in the DNA in that single cell would show up in whatever cells came from it.

Scientists did not start their work manipulating DNA with human cells or the cells of multi-celled plants or animals. They began with the very simplest forms of life—bacteria consisting of one cell and having only a single chromosome. These cells

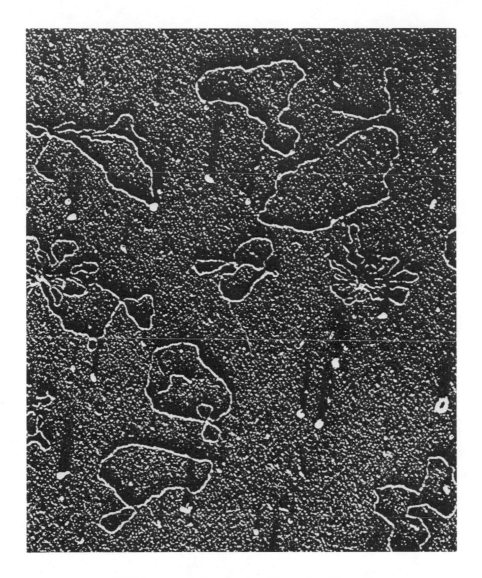

DNA strands in the nucleus of cells and viruses. Each strand, about 10 atoms wide, is magnified about 90,000 times.

divide almost every twenty minutes, and so it is possible to get observable results in a short time.

The work done is much like that of a film editor. Pieces of DNA are identified, then cut out and carefully inserted into the DNA strand of a microbe. All of this work, called *gene splicing,* must be done with material visible only with the magnification of a high-powered microscope. Many scientists are convinced, however, that the engineering of life by gene splicing will bring great benefits to humankind.

When the first successful gene splices were accomplished in the early 1970s and news of the event reached the public, it created a furor greater than was brought about by the splitting of the atom and the development of nuclear weapons. One concern was that scientists would produce an uncontrollable strain of some deadly disease organism. Over the years the fears have been calmed. Regulations and guidelines have been established, and the work goes on.

In 1980, at Guys Hospital in London, England, patients with diabetes were given insulin produced by genetic engineering. An insulin-making DNA code had been spliced into the genetic material of bacteria, which then immediately began producing it. It was believed that the insulin produced in this manner was better and safer than insulin obtained from the traditional sources—the pancreas of a pig or cow. It was an exact chemical copy of human insulin and would be less likely to be rejected or cause side effects. By using these biological factories, insulin could eventually be made available to millions of diabetics more cheaply and more efficiently than ever before.

Genetically engineered microbes will soon be manufacturing drugs, vaccines, hormones, antibodies, and a variety of medical "tools" used in diagnosis. Many of these products will be superior to any that are currently available.

But the rewards of DNA research are not limited to medicine. With genetic engineering, crops that cannot transform nitrogen into a usable form can be made to do so or be made to grow alongside microbes that do the job for them. These crops, including corn, wheat, rice, barley, and other cereal grains, take nutrients from the soil and give nothing back. They demand large amounts of fertilizer or must be alternated with alfalfa, clover, or other legumes that do enrich the soil. Bioengineers are also working to produce crops that are resistant to known diseases and eliminate such devastating livestock killers as foot-and-mouth disease.

To feed the world's hungry, bioengineered microbial products can be added to flour, eggs, and other conventional foods as high-protein extenders. The microbes themselves can be grown on waste materials from paper-making and other industries, helping to clean up the environment while at the same time providing food.

Yeasts can be put to work turning plant wastes into fuel that can operate engines. Bacteria have been targeted to eat oil from spills and other wastes. The list goes on and on.

Clearly, a new world is on the horizon. And it is a world heavily shaped by cells like those that make up your body. The cells themselves are incredibly small and their contents even smaller. But their intricate workings, when understood and manipulated to their best effect, promise to provide us with the power to make our lives better, safer, and more productive.

GLOSSARY

Amino acids. The chief components of proteins. They are synthesized by living cells or obtained by eating protein-rich foods.

Asexual reproduction. Reproduction without the union of individuals, or sex cells.

ATP. Adenosine triphosphate. A chemical produced by an enzyme whose molecules supply energy for many cellular processes.

Axons. Conduct impulses away from a nerve cell body; usually long, single fibers.

Cell membrane. The semipermeable outer layer of the cell body. Molecules of food can pass through this membrane to nourish the cell, and waste products can pass out of it.

Cells. The smallest organized units of living things. All cells contain essentially the same parts, though there are many specialized cells performing many specialized activities. There are two basic kinds of cells—plant cells and animal cells. Only plant cells—some varieties—can make food.

Cell wall. The outermost protective layer of a plant cell.

Centriole. An organelle in the cell's cytoplasm that has a role in cell reproduction.

Chlorophyll. The green matter inside chloroplasts (see entry) that help a plant to make food in a process called *photosynthesis.*

Chloroplasts. Structures floating in the cell's cytoplasm that contain the green substance chlorophyll (see entry). Chloroplasts are the site where food-making (photosynthesis) takes place.

Chromatin. The part of the cell's nucleus that contains the genetic material passed along in reproduction.

Chromosomes. The small bodies made of a nuclear protein that form from the chromatin during the reproduction process. Chromosomes contain the genes (see entry) that pass the characteristics of the cell onto the offspring.

Cytology. The branch of science that deals with the study of cells.

Cytoplasm. The jellylike material in all cells in which the nucleus and other structures float.

Dendrites. Branches of nerve cells that carry impulses from outside the cell toward the body of the cell.

Dermis. The inner layer of the skin where new skin cells are produced. Hair roots are contained in the dermis, and oil is secreted from it.

Diploid number. Body cells that contain the full complement of chromosomes are said to contain the "diploid" number.

DNA. Deoxyribonucleic acid. Nucleic acids that are the basis of heredity in most organisms. The structure of DNA is a double helix, or spiral ladder.

Double helix. See DNA above.

Eggs. The sex cells produced by females. When united with a sperm cell through fertilization, a "zygote" can form—the first stage in the development of a fetus.

Endoplasmic reticulum. A system of interconnected "canals" in the cytoplasm that helps to transport materials within and to and from the cell.

Enzymes. Proteins produced by cells that catalyze biochemical processes, such as digestion, in the body.

Epidermis. The top, or outermost, layer of the skin.

Fertilization. The process whereby two sex cells (egg and sperm) unite to form a zygote—a single cell that will reproduce and eventually become an embryo.

Gametes. Sex cells. See entries for *eggs* and *sperm*.

Gene. A unit, made up of nucleic acid, that carries a particular characteristic of the cell and passes it along to the offspring. Genes contain codes for directing the manufacture of proteins or other genes.

Gene splicing. The act of taking a piece of DNA from one organism and inserting it into the DNA of a second organism, either to manufacture a new substance or change the inherited characteristics of the second organism.

Genetics. The science of heredity, or how genes do their work.

Golgi apparatus. A component in the cell's cytoplasm that plays a role in the manufacture of cell products.

Hemoglobin. An iron-rich oxygen-carrying protein in red blood cells.

Hormones. Products of certain living cells that affect or regulate bodily activities.

Involuntary (smooth) muscles. Muscles that are automatically stimulated into action by nerves and by changes in body chemistry. These muscles are slow to tire and include the heart.

Leucocytes. White blood cells, whose main purpose is to fight bacterial or other infection.

Lymph. The pale fluid that bathes the cells and tissues in the body.

Lysosomes. Saclike organelles in cells. They contain enzymes which aid in digestion.

Meiosis. A type of cell division similar to mitosis except that it occurs with sex cells and results in each cell receiving only half the normal number of chromosomes.

Melanin. A skin pigment causing the skin to appear spotted, brown, or black.

Metabolism. The total of chemical changes in living cells, resulting in the production of energy for growth, repair, and movement.

Mitochondria. Rounded organelles in the cytoplasm that produce energy for the cell through respiration (breathing in of oxygen).

Mitosis. A type of cell division that takes place in the nucleus of the cell and results in two "daughter" offspring, each containing the same number of chromosomes as the parent.

Monoploid (haploid) number. Half the number of chromosomes found in body cells. Sex cells—egg and sperm—each contain the haploid number.

Mutants. Offspring that do not receive the normal number of chromosomes or receive them in the wrong order. A few mutants, or mutations, are better off than their parents, but most are unable to survive successfully.

Nerves. Bands of nerve tissue that connect parts of the nervous system to other organs and conduct nerve impulses. They are made up chiefly of dendrites and axons (see entries).

Neurons. Nerve cells.

Nuclear sap. The clear substance in the cell nucleus.

Nucleoli. Small, spherical bodies in the cell. They contain RNA and are associated with cell reproduction.

Nucleus. The cell's control center, an organelle essential to cell reproduction and protein synthesis. The nucleus is composed of nuclear sap and complex nucleoproteins from which chromosomes arise.

Organelles. Special structures suspended in the cytoplasm of a cell. Different organelles serve different purposes.

Organs. Parts of the body, such as the heart, stomach, and so on, composed of different types of cell tissue all working together to perform a specific function.

Osteocytes. Bone cells that produce new bone cells and secrete a protein material in which minerals are deposited.

Platelets. Disc-like blood cells that aid in blood clotting.

Red blood cells. Hemoglobin-containing blood cells that carry oxygen to the tissues and are responsible for the red color of blood.

Reproduction. The act or process by which plants and animals give rise to offspring.

Ribosomes. Granules in the cytoplasm containing RNA, a substance aiding in the synthesis of protein and associated with heredity and cell reproduction.

RNA. Ribonucleic acid. Nucleic acids that are associated with important cellular chemical activities and work with DNA in protein synthesis and cell reproduction.

Sexual reproduction. Reproduction with two parents, each of whom contributes half the normal number of chromosomes to the zygote.

Sperm. The male sex cell, which, during fertilization, unites with the egg, the female sex cell, to form the zygote.

Synapse. The point at which a nerve impulse jumps from one neuron, or nerve cell, to another.

Systems. Groups of body organs, all working together to accomplish a specific purpose. For example, the digestive system's purpose is to make food usable by the cells.

Tissues. Groups of similar cells working together and forming the structural materials of plants and animals.

Vacuoles. Small cavities containing fluids and other substances in the cytoplasm of cells.

Voluntary (skeletal or striated) muscles. Muscles over whose movements we have conscious control. These contain bands of protein that make the cells looked striped. Voluntary muscles are capable of quick movement but tire easily.

White blood cells. Blood cells that contain no hemoglobin.

Zygote. The cell formed from the union of two sex cells, or gametes. From this single cell comes the fetus that eventually becomes a fully formed individual.

INDEX